HEALTHY CITIES: IMPROVING URBAN LIFE

UNDERSTANDING GLOBAL ISSUES

Published by Smart Apple Media
1980 Lookout Drive
North Mankato, Minnesota 56003
USA

Library of Congress Cataloging-in-Publication Data

Lomberg, Michelle.
Healthy cities : improving urban life / Michelle Lomberg.
    p. cm. -- (Understanding global issues)
Summary: Examines the urbanization of the world's population, discussing
the growth of megacities, model city planing, projects and plans that
deal with clean water and proper sanitation, the health of city
residents, and the urban economy.
Includes bibliographical references and index.
  ISBN 1-58340-359-0 (Library Bound : alk. paper)
  1. Cities and towns--Juvenile literature. 2. Urbanization--Juvenile
literature. 3. Urban health--Juvenile literature. 4. Quality of
life--Juvenile literature. [1. Cities and towns. 2. Urbanization. 3.
Urban health. 4. Quality of life.] I. Title.
  HT151.L62 2004
  307.76--dc21

                              2003000112
                           Printed in Malaysia
                           2 4 6 8 9 7 5 3 1

EDITOR Donald Wells **COPY EDITOR** Frances Purslow
TEXT ADAPTATION Michelle Lomberg **DESIGNER** Terry Paulhus
PHOTO RESEARCHERS Tracey Carruthers and Peggy Chan
LAYOUT Terry Paulhus **SERIES EDITOR** Jennifer Nault
CREATIVE COMPANY EDITOR Jill Weingartz

$22.00

Smart Apple/ Bond

11-19-04

Contents

Introduction

The movement of people from rural areas to cities is called urbanization. The urbanization of the world's population may be the biggest social change in history. The number of urban dwellers has grown quickly. In 1900, about 14 percent of the world's people lived in cities. Today, that number has increased to nearly 50 percent. Rapid growth of cities will continue. By 2030, the urban population is expected to reach 60 percent—a total of five billion people. Many of these people will be poor. Seventy-seven percent of them will live in **developing countries**.

Urbanization is often seen as a negative phenomenon. Large cities are linked with overcrowding, slums, traffic jams, pollution, and crime. Some governments try to discourage urbanization. Such policies have proven useless. The World Health Organization (WHO) recognizes the importance of urbanization, and WHO's Healthy Cities Program attempts to deal with the health and social costs of urbanization.

Lack of affordable housing near major employment centers and urban sprawl are just two factors that lead to traffic jams.

The World Bank also recognizes the importance of urbanization and is optimistic about cities. There are many reasons for this optimism. For example, technology is making access to communications and electrical power easier. Also, more people are concerned about human rights and the environment, and urban dwellers have become more involved in projects aimed toward improving life in cities. To help improve the quality of life in cities, the World Bank sponsors a number of projects

> ### Urbanization is the movement of people from rural areas to cities.

that help cities cope with the pressures of growth.

Despite some disadvantages, people who live in cities are generally better off than those who live in rural areas. City dwellers have better access to education, health care, and jobs. As a country becomes more urbanized, its gross domestic product (GDP) per person tends to improve.

Organizations such as WHO and the World Bank understand that a healthy city means more

than just the physical health of its citizens. It refers to complete physical, mental, and social well being. Too often, however, urban people do not feel good about themselves or their cities. In **developed countries**, people complain about traffic jams, low self-esteem, and violence. In developing countries, people are concerned about a lack of clean water, proper **sanitation**, decent housing, clean air, and jobs.

The United Nations (UN) is the largest organization that deals with cities. It plays a valuable role in social and economic development around the world, and various UN agencies are involved in improving urban life. These agencies include the UN Development Program, the World Health Organization, and the UN Center for Human Settlements.

Although development has often been held back by the desire of central governments to control a city's power and money, getting central government and city authorities to work together is a task for which the UN is well suited. The UN also tries to involve community residents, independent experts, and technology specialists in its projects designed to improve urban life.

People and Urbanization

There are many reasons for the increase in urbanization. In 18th-century England, people moved from the countryside to cities for two main reasons. The first reason was a change in property law. This change made it difficult for people who did not own land to find places for their animals to graze. The second reason was the Industrial Revolution, which created jobs in mills and factories in England's cities.

There are many reasons for increased urbanization.

As people were forced to leave their rural lives, they flocked to cities. Newcomers to cities often found themselves in unhealthy working and living conditions.

Similar changes have occurred around the world, and today, people migrate for many of the same reasons. Cities offer higher wages and access to services not available in rural areas. With the increase in urban populations, today's cities face the same challenges as their 18th-

At the beginning of the 19th century, 2.5 percent of the world's population lived in urban settings. This number is expected to climb to 60 percent by 2030.

and 19th-century counterparts. Cities must provide food, water, sanitation, services, education, and jobs for long-time residents and new arrivals.

One symbol of global urbanization is the mega-city. Mega-cities have populations of 10 million or more. There were only five mega-cities in the world in 1975, but by 2001, there were 17 mega-cities. The UN estimates that there might be as many as 27 mega-cities by 2015. The vast majority of mega-cities will be in the developing world, with more than half of them in Asia. The UN estimates that by 2015, Dhaka, Bangladesh, will have 22.8 million residents; Sao Paulo, Brazil, will have 21.2 million residents; and Jakarta, Indonesia, will have more than 17 million residents.

UNITED NATIONS HUMAN DEVELOPMENT INDEX

Overall HDI rank	Life expectancy rank	Education rank	GDP per capita rank
1. Norway	1. Japan	1. Belgium	1. Luxembourg
2. Australia	2. Sweden	2. United Kingdom	2. *United States*
3. Canada	3. Hong Kong, China	3. Finland	3. Norway
4. Sweden	4. Iceland	4. Australia	4. Iceland
5. Belgium	5. Australia	5. The Netherlands	5. Switzerland
6. *United States*	6. Switzerland	6. Sweden	6. Canada
7. Iceland	7. Canada	7. New Zealand	7. Ireland
8. The Netherlands	8. Israel	8. Denmark	8. Denmark
9. Japan	9. Italy	9. Canada	9. Belgium
10. Finland	10. France	10. Norway	10. Austria
	25. *United States*	11. *United States*	

The United Nations Human Development Index (HDI) measures a country's achievements. While the gross domestic product (GDP) and gross national product (GNP) are used to measure the economic health of a country, the HDI measures how people really live. The higher the HDI number, the less poverty a country experiences. In order to determine this, the HDI measures three main aspects of human development: longevity, knowledge, and standard of living. Longevity refers to a person's life expectancy at birth. Knowledge measures school enrollment and adult literacy. The standard of living is measured by GDP **per capita**.

HPI rank (developed countries)	
1. Sweden	6. Germany
2. Norway	7. Luxembourg
3. The Netherlands	8. France
4. Finland	9. Japan
5. Denmark	10. Spain
	17. *United States*

Many people live in poverty. They do not enjoy a long life, have access to good education, or achieve a decent standard of living. The Human Poverty Index (HPI) measures a country's poverty using the same three aspects of human development as the HDI: longevity, knowledge, and standard of living. Of all developed countries, the U.S. ranks 17th on the HPI.

Social and economic development is promoted by urbanization. As urbanization progresses, a country's GNP and UN HDI ranking improve. Cities provide more business for farmers, which improves life for those in rural areas. Urbanization reduces population growth by providing more opportunities for women.

Much thought and energy have been given to learning how to improve cities. There is now wide agreement on how to manage cities successfully. Six key elements have been identified:

1. **Decentralization**—Cities should be allowed to govern themselves, and they should have full support from the central government.
2. **Community Participation**—Citizens' involvement in local government is important to good city management.
3. **Economic Opportunity**—Jobs should be created for all skill levels. This would reduce poverty.
4. **Infrastructure**—Cities need roads, sanitation, transportation, water, and power. Private companies and governments should work together to provide these services.
5. Land Rights—Cities must balance private investment in land with ecological concerns.
6. Municipal Finances—Taxing and spending should be fair, and information about taxes and how they are spent should be made available to the public.

Cities around the world show that these principles make good practical sense. Some examples are Curitiba, Brazil; Puerta Princesa, Philippines; and Cox's Bazaar, Bangladesh.

Although decentralization has helped to improve life in many cities around the world, it does not work for all cities. For example, in the United States, city planning is mostly decentralized. Each city bears the cost of its own infrastructure and

CURITIBA, BRAZIL

Curitiba, Brazil, is a triumph of city planning. Urbanization brought rapid growth to the city. In the 1950s, there were only 150,000 people living in Curitiba. Today, it has 1.6 million residents. When planning to meet the needs of urbanization, Curitiba's leaders considered the environment and the needs of the people. Their policies have resulted in less pollution and litter. In order to fight air pollution, the city developed one of the best public transit systems in the world. There are car-free streets downtown and many parks and bicycle paths. Most of Curitiba's trash is recycled. Poor families can exchange their trash for bus tickets or food. Businesses provide food and wages for homeless children. Its sensitive planning has made Curitiba a model for cities trying to cope with the pressures of urbanization.

KEY CONCEPTS

GDP (Gross Domestic Product)
The gross domestic product is the total value of goods produced and services provided in a country in one year. GDP is used to measure the wealth of a country. Some economists argue that GDP does not tell the whole story. For example, GDP measures the amount of lumber sold, but it does not take into account the environmental damage caused by logging.

Industrial Revolution The Industrial Revolution began in England in the 1700s. Manufacturers started using machines to produce items traditionally made by hand. Cotton fabric was one of the first industrially produced goods.

As the Industrial Revolution spread to the United States and European countries, it changed the economies of these countries. Traditionally, people had worked at home. Usually, they made or grew their own goods to sell. Often, they were paid to make goods for larger businesses to sell. After the Industrial Revolution, people worked on machines in services. This leaves little money for helping people. In many city centers, people must deal with job and housing shortages. With the loss of jobs and housing, people have been abandoning city centers and moving to suburbs. They believe suburbs are safer and offer better opportunities. As neighborhoods in city centers are left to decay, suburbs indeed become better places to live.

In 1999, the U.S. government proposed a plan for cities and suburbs that it hopes will improve conditions in city centers. This plan for cities has four parts:

1. Employers will be encouraged to hire unemployed and **underemployed** people.
2. The government will provide more job training.
3. More affordable housing will be available.
4. Inner-city communities will be improved.

This proposal by the U.S. government is designed to improve the quality of life in depressed city centers and encourage better relationships between cities and suburbs. The authors of this plan hope that city centers will share in the **prosperity** enjoyed by the rest of the country.

▓▓▓ **Many cities are improving the condition of their city centers in order to stop the migration of people and jobs to suburbs.**

factories. They were usually paid very low wages and worked long hours in dangerous conditions.

Levels of government In the U.S., there are three main levels of government: national, state, and local. The national, or federal, government is the government of the United States. Each state also has its own government. Local government is a partnership of county and **municipal** governments. Each level of government has its own responsibilities. Some responsibilities are shared by all three levels of government.

United Nations (UN) The UN is a group of 191 countries working together to solve global problems. The UN was founded in 1945, just after the end of World War II. Its goals are to maintain world peace, develop friendly relations among nations, encourage nations to cooperate in order to solve international problems, and promote respect for human rights.

City Food and Water

A fast-growing city may find it hard to meet its citizens' basic needs: food and water. Providing clean water has long been a major goal of the World Health Organization. The United Nations named the 1980s the International Drinking Water Supply and Sanitation Decade. During this decade, more than one billion people were provided with clean water. Sanitation was made available for 770 million people. In the 1990s, an additional 816 million people gained access to fresh water, and 747 million were provided with sanitation. However, these measures cannot keep up with population growth. Today, more than one billion people lack clean water, and more than two billion people do not have proper sanitation. The majority of people without safe water and proper sanitation live in Asia. In North America, practically everyone has clean water and proper sanitation.

People in cities are more likely than rural dwellers to have access to clean water and proper sanitation. In 1990, 85 percent of the developing world's urban population had access to clean water, and more than 70 percent had proper sanitation. Numbers in rural areas were much lower. While almost 60 percent of rural dwellers had clean water, only 40 percent had proper sanitation.

In 2000, the figures improved for cities in developing countries, but they became worse for rural areas. Clean water was provided to more than 90 percent of urban dwellers, and more than 85 percent had proper sanitation. Clean water reached more than 70 percent of rural dwellers, but less than 40 percent had proper sanitation.

WHO regards clean water and proper sanitation as the basis of good health. By 2015, WHO's goal is to provide clean water to more than 90 percent of the world's people, and proper

People in developing nations often have a difficult time finding water that is not contaminated and must make do with water sources that may be unsafe.

WATER, SANITATION, AND HEALTH

In developing countries, 80 percent of illnesses are water-related. Approximately 34,000 people die every day from water-related diseases. Untreated water can be a breeding ground for insects that carry disease, and if water is **contaminated** by sewage, it can carry bacteria. Waterborne bacteria cause **cholera**, **hepatitis**, and other diseases, and food washed or prepared with contaminated water can also cause illness. Adequate sanitation ensures that sewage is properly treated and kept away from the water supply. Providing people with clean water and proper sanitation saves countless lives.

sanitation to more than 80 percent. In order to reach this goal, water will need to be supplied to another one billion people in cities, and almost six million in rural areas. Proper sanitation will have to be brought to one billion urbanites and one billion rural dwellers. This target will be difficult to reach because a small amount of international aid must cover many development projects.

The cost of providing these basic services seems to be great. Approximately $134 billion was spent in the 1980s, with one-third of this money provided by international aid. Over the past decade, about $16 billion has been spent each year to build new water and sanitation facilities. This may seem like a large sum of money, but it should be noted that Europeans spend $11 billion each year just on ice cream. Americans and Europeans spend $17 billion per year on pet food. Compared to these items, water and sanitation are relatively inexpensive. It should be possible for everyone to have a safe water supply and proper sanitation.

A good supply of clean water and proper sanitation are signs of a healthy city. Another sign of a healthy city is reflected in the cost of food.

> ***WHO regards clean water and proper sanitation as the basis of good health.***

If an average citizen has to spend half of his or her income on food, not much money is left to cover other necessities. In prosperous cities such as New York City, New York; London, England; or Sydney, Australia, about 15 percent of the average household budget is used to buy food. In poor cities such as Lagos, Nigeria, or Dhaka, Bangladesh, more than 60 percent of household income is spent on food.

Millions of people have little hope of getting beyond the subsistence level, which means barely meeting one's basic needs. Still, some people believe urbanization can improve the lives of the poor. Singapore is an example of a city helped by urbanization and good planning. Singapore was once a collection of poor slums. Today, it is a

---

Millions of people live at the subsistence level.

---

sleek, high-tech city. Singapore's leaders have emphasized planning, education, infrastructure, and a free market system.

The free market system has gained wide acceptance since the fall of **communism**. An example of this system is when food grown outside a city is sold to city dwellers in street markets. However, such markets are never entirely free of controls. For example, there must be controls to ensure that food is clean. WHO runs a program to help food handlers and sellers practice good hygiene. Government inspectors are urged to give advice rather than penalties. In this way, market workers learn how to safely handle food and dispose of waste.

One example of what can be done to improve food supply to the urban poor is the PAIS program (*Programa Alimentario Integral y Solidario*, which means Communal Whole Foods Program) of Buenos Aires, Argentina. This program brings together the regional government, local nongovernmental organizations (NGOs), and community members to help the city's poor. The PAIS program has three stages. First, community kitchens of 20 to 100 residents are set up. Second, the program provides flour, seeds, and equipment for producing food. Third, the program helps the kitchen groups organize small businesses such as vegetable gardens, food processing plants, and food distribution networks. Experts are studying the PAIS program to see if it would work in other countries.

In U.S. cities, organizations such as America's Second Harvest help provide food to the poor. America's Second Harvest is a network of food banks and food-rescue programs. These

THE PHAST APPROACH

The Participatory Hygiene and Sanitation Transformation (PHAST) approach helps communities in the developing world improve sanitation. This approach encourages citizens to get involved in solving local water, sanitation, and disease control problems. The community looks at its own beliefs and practices and decides what needs to be changed. Outside experts also participate and share information with the community. These experts include local health workers, water and sanitation engineers, and social scientists.

The PHAST approach was created because traditional health education methods were not working. It is based on the following principles:

- Communities can and should make their own plans for disease prevention.
- Communities have traditional and modern knowledge about health.
- When people understand how better sanitation will help them, they will act.
- All people can understand that sewage carries disease.
- Communities can identify ways to stop the spread of disease.

programs receive donations of food, and agencies and charities distribute this food to the poor. In 2001, 1.7 billion pounds (771 million kg) of food was distributed to more than 23 million U.S. citizens in need.

Community gardens are another way to provide food. They are also good for the environment. In some parts of Africa, migrants from the countryside operate urban mini-farms. Many U.S. cities have community gardens, too. The Care Assurance System for the Aging and Homebound (CASA) community garden in Huntsville, Alabama, grows food for the community's senior citizens. In 2001, the garden yielded more than 19,000 pounds (8,600 kg) of vegetables. Volunteers harvested the crop, and the food was donated to more than 7,500 senior citizens in Huntsville and the surrounding county. The CASA community garden is planted and tended by more than 1,000 volunteers.

In the United States, 36 percent of people using food banks have had to choose between buying food and paying for housing. As a result, food banks are strained.

The World Health Organization is responsible for helping everyone attain the highest level of health. Its headquarters are located in Geneva, Switzerland.

KEY CONCEPTS

Food bank, food rescue Food banks are centers where people can go to receive free food. Most food banks are run by volunteers, and the food is donated by businesses, charities, and individuals. Food-rescue programs collect food that would otherwise be thrown away. The food is usually donated by businesses such as bakeries, restaurants, and grocery stores. The rescued food is then distributed through food banks.

Free market system In a free market system, businesses compete with each other for customers. The government does not control prices, and there is no government aid for failing businesses. Competitive tactics include lowering prices and buying competing businesses. In an ideal free market system, there are no controls or regulations. In reality, however, there is no perfectly free market. In the United States, for example, the law prevents companies from buying up all of their competitors.

International aid International aid is money given by developed countries to help developing countries. Aid money is usually used for development or emergency relief. At the 1992 Earth Summit, developed countries agreed to spend 0.7 percent of their budgets on international aid. Few countries are meeting this target.

Nongovernmental organizations (NGOs) Nongovernmental organizations are non-profit agencies that are independent from government. NGO projects usually deal with community development, social services, protecting the environment, and helping the poor. NGOs are often staffed by volunteers.

World Health Organization (WHO) WHO is the United Nations agency for health. It was established in 1948. The goal of WHO is to achieve the highest possible level of health for everyone. For WHO, health is not just the absence of disease. Health includes complete physical, mental, and social well being. WHO works with governments and NGOs to promote and carry out effective health policies.

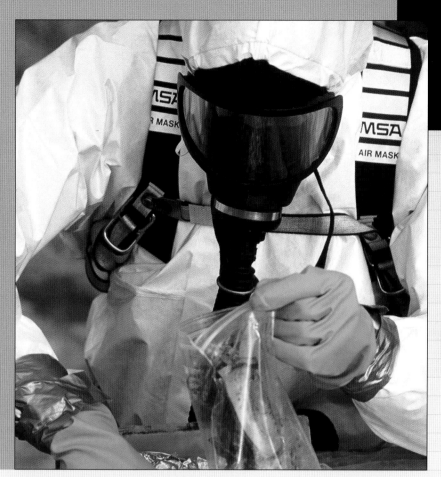

Environmental Health Professional

Duties: Prevents and eliminates public health hazards
Education: Bachelor's degree, preferably in environmental health
Interests: Science, math, health care

Navigate to **www.neha.org** for more information about environmental health professionals. Also click on **www.niehs.nih.gov** for information about the field of environmental health.

Careers in Focus

Environmental health professionals keep living environments safe for people. Their work covers a wide range of jobs. It can involve designing water and sanitation systems or pest control programs. It may concern food safety or hazardous materials. Environmental health professionals work to make homes, workplaces, and public spaces safe and healthy. The environmental health professional must be knowledgeable in many subjects, including law, disease control, workplace safety, hazardous materials and radiation, and disaster response.

Environmental health professionals do a variety of different jobs. **Practitioners** may work in the field taking samples or performing inspections and evaluations. They may work in an office writing reports. They may work with scientists, government officials, or community groups. They may even handle hazardous materials. Many environmental health professionals work in county health departments.

Registered environmental health specialists are certified by the National Environmental Health Association. In order to be certified, candidates must pass an exam. Candidates should have a Bachelor's, Master's, or doctoral degree in environmental health. Candidates can also take the exam if they have a Bachelor's degree in another subject. However, they must have taken math, science, and environmental engineering courses. They also need two years of work experience in the environmental health field.

Waste Management

Cities produce vast amounts of waste. All cities need adequate systems for dealing with sewage and household waste. Without these types of systems, no city can be healthy.

In the developed world, citizens expect their taxes to cover the cost of waste removal and disposal. For most residents, garbage is collected every week or two, and it is taken away to isolated disposal sites. For most people in developed countries, waste is largely "out of sight, out of mind."

In developing countries, waste is all too visible. It is often left to pile up on the streets because no one can afford to pay for its removal. Scavengers take all of the useful items, and the rest is left to rot. Materials such as plastic do not rot. They pile up, and any attempts to burn them result in harmful smoke.

In developing countries, waste management programs are often poorly run due to a lack of resources. Garbage trucks are often out of service because they have not been maintained. In 1987, Dar es Salaam, Tanzania, bought 30 new garbage trucks.

Sanitary landfills are the most common form of waste disposal in the United States.

By 1992, only three were still running. The rest had been used for spare parts.

Similar stories come from other cities. Politicians are often eager to win support by spending money on services such as waste management. International aid

---

A healthy city will have an adequate system for dealing with sewage and household waste.

---

agencies also donate money to highly visible projects. However, this type of spending must come with a long-term plan because the efficient operation of a waste management system over several years is a complex job. Waste management requires more than just money. Organization and commitment are needed, as

well as a corruption-free environment. Some cities are privatizing waste collection. Private waste management companies are motivated by profit to do a good job.

Corruption is a problem in waste management. In some cities, waste management companies bribe city officials to get contracts. These bribes can account for 10 to 30 percent of waste contract costs. Corruption can be reduced by making the process of bidding for contracts more transparent and open and holding city officials accountable for the contracts they award.

The use of different private companies in different zones of a city is another way to fight corruption. Cities such as Bogotá, Colombia, and Phoenix, Arizona, use this approach to solve the problem of corruption. Phoenix uses more than one company for its waste services.

THE MEGA-CITIES PROJECT

The Mega-Cities Project was established in 1987. The project unites leaders from communities, governments, businesses, universities, and media. Its focus is to share solutions to urban problems such as waste management. The project has research teams in 22 cities around the world. These teams work on improving the economic, environmental, and social life of cities. The activities of the Mega-Cities Project include sharing ideas about urban problems, training present and future community leaders, and doing research on urban issues. Two U.S. cities, New York and Los Angeles, are part of the Mega-Cities Project. They are expected to be mega-cities by 2015.

One company is used for collecting garbage; another for collecting, recycling, sorting, and selling recycled materials; and a third company for operating recycling facilities.

Hazardous waste is a growing problem in some developing countries. City garbage may contain toxic materials such as batteries, insect sprays, glues, and cleaning fluids. Ideally, toxic waste should be separated from safe waste. However, even in developed countries, this does not always happen. In developing countries, mixed waste is often piled close to communities and water sources, which can contaminate the water supply.

Waste cannot always be recycled. It is sometimes incinerated (burned at high

SCAVENGERS

Scavengers are a common sight in cities around the world. Many poor and homeless people earn money by collecting recyclable waste such as bottles and scrap metal. In Cairo, Egypt, the Zabbaleen people have collected garbage for centuries. In 1980, their efforts gained official recognition. The Zabbaleen community has formed a partnership with the city of Cairo and international donors. Cairo has donated land for the Zabbaleen to use as storage and sorting areas. Non-profit organizations provide the Zabbaleen with training, equipment, and money to start businesses. These businesses sell goods made from recycled materials, including shoes, textiles, and tinware. This project creates jobs and income for the Zabbaleen people and improves waste collection in Cairo.

temperatures). Technology exists to control dangerous **emissions** created by burning garbage. This method is used more and more in the developed world. Unfortunately, few developing countries can afford incinerators or emission-control technology. Cities in China, for example, have much more air pollution than U.S. cities. The air pollution in Chinese cities is made worse by the fact that they burn coal for energy.

> *The technology to reduce air pollution exists, but governments must be willing to take action.*

Air pollution can be controlled. When London, England, banned the burning of coal, it reduced the smog that threatened the health of its residents. California has made laws to increase the number of **zero-emission** vehicles on its roads. The technology to reduce air pollution exists, but leaders from all levels of government must be willing to take action.

WHERE DOES WASTE GO?

In the United States, waste is disposed of in a number of ways.

Landfills
Landfills are huge pits that hold garbage. Eighty percent of waste in the U.S. is sent to landfills. Landfills in many cities are too full to use, so these communities must ship their trash to other locations. For example, garbage from New Jersey is sent to New Mexico for disposal. Although they are the most common form of waste disposal, landfills have problems. Methane gas can build up and explode. Bad-smelling or even toxic fumes can escape, and waste can contaminate water and soil around landfills. Rats and other pests thrive in landfills. Recently, many improvements have been made to landfill technology. Plastic liners prevent leakage and contamination, and new technologies control the buildup of methane gas.

Deep-well injection
The Environmental Protection Agency (EPA) banned the disposal of liquid waste in landfills in 1984. Today, liquid waste is injected into wells deep below sources of drinking water. Liners separate the waste from the soil and ground water. However, if the well is poorly constructed or maintained, waste may still leak into drinking water.

Incinerators
Incinerators burn garbage. In the 1960s and 1970s, incinerators were blamed for polluting the air. Today, incinerators have devices to control pollution. However, there are still concerns about the toxic chemicals and ash from incinerators that are sent to landfills.

Reduce, reuse, recycle—the three Rs
By far, the best way to manage waste is to reduce, reuse, and recycle. There are many examples of the three Rs in practice. For example, waste can be reduced simply by carrying groceries in reusable bags. Manufacturers are finding ways to reuse plastics to make fleece clothing. Cities across the U.S. and around the world have curbside recycling programs. By practicing the three Rs, individuals can take control of waste management.

In sanitary landfills, garbage is spread out in thin layers and compacted by a bulldozer. When approximately 10 feet (3 m) of garbage has been compacted, it is covered with a thin layer of clean soil.

KEY CONCEPTS

Privatization Privatization means that private companies provide services that were once delivered by government. Privatization can take many forms. For example, a government can award a franchise, or exclusive contract, to one service provider, or government and private service providers may compete for contracts. In some cases, services are taken over by volunteers or community organizations.

City Planner

Duties: Organizes land use in cities and neighborhoods
Education: Degree in planning
Interests: Research, report writing, creating maps and models

Navigate to BLS Career Information **www.bls.gov/k12/html/soc_005. htm** for more information about planning and related careers. Also click on **www.wikipedia.org/wiki/ Urban_planner** to learn more about urban planners.

Careers in Focus

City planners decide how land will be used in a city. They recommend locations for houses, schools, businesses, and parks. They also plan how services, such as water and sanitation, will be delivered. Planners may also make suggestions about protecting environmentally sensitive areas, such as wetlands, rivers, or forests. They are involved in every aspect of city life, from the building and planning of concert halls to sewers.

Most planners spend much of their time in the office. Their work may begin with research into the history, ecology, and population of an area.

Planners work as part of a team with city leaders, community members, and various experts. Often, planners visit the sites they are working on to observe the area's features. They write reports and prepare maps and models on a computer.

In the U.S., planners must be certified by the American Institute of Certified Planners (AICP). In order to become certified, candidates must pass an AICP exam, but first, they must have a combination of educational qualifications and work experience. Candidates with a Master's degree must have two years' experience, while those with a Bachelor's degree need three years' experience. People without a college degree require eight years' experience.

Serving the People

Cities should benefit those who live in them. Unfortunately, it is often difficult for a city to solve all of its problems and meet the needs of every resident.

One way of dealing with urban problems is with a top-down approach. With this approach, solutions are agreed upon by bankers and experts and imposed on communities. Top-down solutions to urban problems do not always work as well as expected.

Since top-down solutions do not always solve a city's problems, advisors have gradually turned to grassroots methods. These methods encourage more involvement from local communities. Governments sometimes resist such movements because they see grassroots groups as a threat to their power.

There may be good reasons for governments to fear grassroots groups and the possible loss of power to cities or municipalities. Some people believe that large cities could replace nations as the power centers of the future. In many countries, a single large city dominates the economy. Singapore is a good example. Once a poor urban area, Singapore became rich by careful planning. It has been voted the "world's best city for business" 10 years in a row. Other **metropolitan** regions enjoy a similar status. For example, New York City, New York; Tokyo, Japan; Hong Kong, China; Cairo, Egypt; and the areas surrounding these cities have a great deal of political and economic influence.

Despite the concerns of national governments, urban leaders are doing all they can to improve cities. City managers connect with each other in a way that was never possible in the past. They share ideas at international conferences and on the Internet. There are global and regional networks that deal with everything from urban crime prevention to waste water treatment. These networks may exist between governments. Other networks are the private projects of nongovernmental

CLEAN ENERGY

Cities need plenty of energy. Houses require light, heat, and air conditioning. Businesses need to operate equipment. Power is also required for public services such as transportation and streetlights. Many countries, including the U.S., rely on fossil fuels for energy. These fuels cannot be replaced, and when they are burned, they cause pollution. Healthy cities around the world are looking for cleaner sources of energy. The best energy sources are renewable and non-polluting.

- Solar energy can be used to heat and light buildings and to heat hot water. Solar energy can also be collected by special panels and converted to electricity.

- Wind power is captured by giant windmills called turbines. This power is turned into electricity. Many city energy providers across the U.S. provide wind-generated energy to their customers.

- Geothermal energy uses steam from hot underground streams. This steam turns a turbine that generates electricity.

- Hydroelectric energy uses running water to rotate turbines.

These clean sources of energy do not use up Earth's resources, and they do not pollute the air.

organizations (NGOs) or groups of individuals.

Also, development projects have changed over the years. Development projects used to focus on specific problems. These projects looked for technical solutions to energy shortages, lack of clean water, the prevention of disease, and overpopulation. Today, development is approached in a more **holistic** way. The holistic approach attempts to balance technology with human needs. While this approach is a big step forward, it is also challenging because development agencies that use a holistic approach can come into conflict with governments that want to maintain control of cities.

Many experts call for more community participation in development projects. They believe more can be achieved

---

Cities should benefit those who live in them.

---

when local people are involved in projects that try to improve the health of a community. This is often difficult, however, because community participation requires strong leadership to ensure that the concerns of various interest groups are addressed.

Interest groups may include businesses, communities, and various levels of government. When these groups try to work together, there can be conflict. Governments may be considered bureaucratic or corrupt. Business may be seen as greedy or uncaring. Community leaders might seem narrow-minded. It can take months or even years to establish trust and respect among these interest groups.

In an effort to reduce air pollution, the city of San Francisco, California, famous for its electric cable cars, buys only zero-emission and ultra-low emission vehicles for public service.

Bringing interest groups together takes effort. Some of the most effective urban programs have been led by strong mayors. Other programs have been helped by outside groups such as NGOs or the UN.

Whoever provides the leadership, it is vital to attract those at the grassroots level. Experts and mayors come and go, but the residents of a city remain. Unless local people are committed to a project, it will not work. If community members do not trust their government, they may refuse to pay taxes. A tax rebellion could stall attempts to bring in services such as electricity or water. Building trust between government and citizens is necessary for good urban management, and for trust to develop, the link between taxes and urban services must be evident.

Electricity is a key service for urban dwellers. Without electricity, it is difficult to work after dark, and children must do their homework by candle or lamplight. Also, families are cut off from radio and television, which provide them with news and entertainment.

In developing countries, governments may not provide electricity to urban slums. In such cases, residents often risk their lives trying to tap into lines illegally. Some may burn fuels such as coal and kerosene for light and heat. These fuels produce unhealthy fumes in the home. Problems such as these are solved when communities make their own electricity.

Solar panels enable communities to make their own electricity. **Solar power** also eliminates dangerous power lines. Unfortunately, solar power alone cannot provide enough electricity for everyone. Developing countries will continue to depend on fossil fuel power stations.

Public transportation is another key issue in cities.

▦ **Hydroelectric power in the U.S., which rose from 16 billion kilowatts in 1920 to 305.6 billion kilowatts in 1999, accounts for eight percent of electric power used in the United States.**

Effective transit systems allow people to live without cars. This conserves fuel and reduces traffic and pollution.

Government planners tend to favor large projects that benefit business or the rich. In the developing world, much emphasis is often placed on roads and cars, even though most of the population cannot afford to drive. In Jakarta, Indonesia, a change in transport policy put 60,000 **rickshaw** drivers out of work. As a result, a nonpolluting form of transportation and a famous tradition were lost.

In India, oxcarts, donkey carts, and human-drawn vehicles are widely used. City planners usually ignore these traditional forms of transport when making plans for future roadways. Politicians who want to seem modern may find it hard to appreciate traditional methods of transportation.

Public-private partnerships can be effective in transport systems. In some German cities, public transit tickets can also be used for taxis in off-peak hours. In Singapore, the same tickets are used for subways and private buses. Passengers' use of tickets is recorded electronically, and the income is divided between bus and subway operators. Seven private bus companies serve New York City commuters. The City of New York owns most of the buses, and it pays for part of the operating costs.

Healthy cities have developed public transport systems using light rail, subways, and buses. These systems replace private cars as the normal mode of urban transport. Cities that focused on the car now regret the choice.

SMART GROWTH

Smart growth is one way for U.S. cities to meet the challenges of growth. Urbanization does not have to bring traffic problems, poverty, and crime. Supporters of smart growth believe in increasing jobs, wages, family time, and success in school. Smart growth favors certain kinds of development.

Economically smart
Smart growth does not require large tax increases. It builds on what already exists.

Environmentally smart
Smart growth protects air quality, water quality, and open space.

Socially smart
Smart growth brings together citizens, governments, and businesses to solve problems.

Smart growth efforts have spread across the United States. New Jersey has established the Garden State Preservation Trust, which will use $1 billion to preserve one million acres (400,000 ha) of farmland, greenways, and open space. The city of Tucson, Arizona, has designed a neighborhood of energy-saving homes. In Fort Collins, Colorado, builders of environmentally friendly buildings receive building permits more quickly.

KEY CONCEPTS

Corruption Government corruption is a serious problem, particularly in the developing world. Corruption often takes the form of bribes. Officials may demand payment in exchange for contracts and permits. Corruption is most common in the areas of construction and sanitation.

Grassroots movements
Governments can be resistant to change and slow to act. In such cases, citizens often unite to demand reforms. Members of grassroots movements organize protests and try to change laws. They draw international attention to their causes, and their actions can force governments to make important changes.

Mapping Urbanization

Figure 1: Urbanization by Country

The world is becoming more urbanized.
In 2000, nearly 50 percent of the world's
population lived in cities.

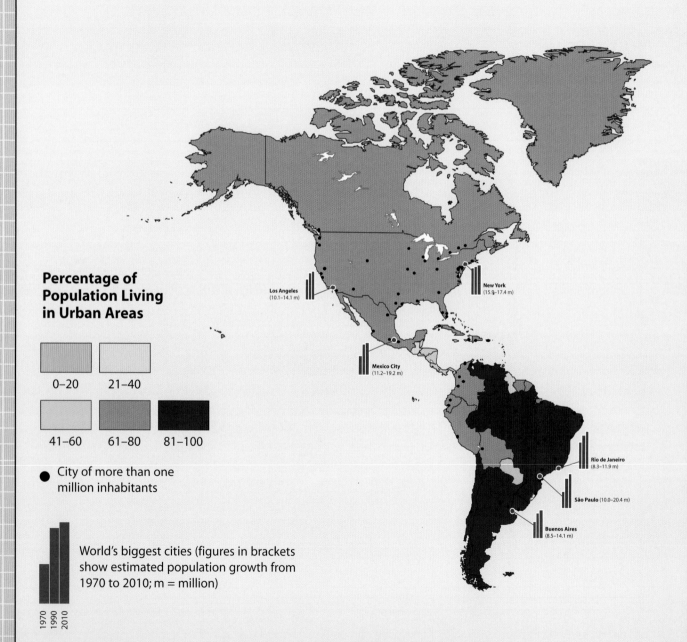

**Percentage of
Population Living
in Urban Areas**

0–20   21–40

41–60   61–80   81–100

● City of more than one
million inhabitants

World's biggest cities (figures in brackets
show estimated population growth from
1970 to 2010; m = million)

1970 1990 2010

Los Angeles
(10.1–14.1 m)

New York
(15.9–17.4 m)

Mexico City
(11.2–19.2 m)

Rio de Janeiro
(8.3–11.9 m)

São Paulo (10.0–20.4 m)

Buenos Aires
(8.5–14.1 m)

Scale 1:93,310,000

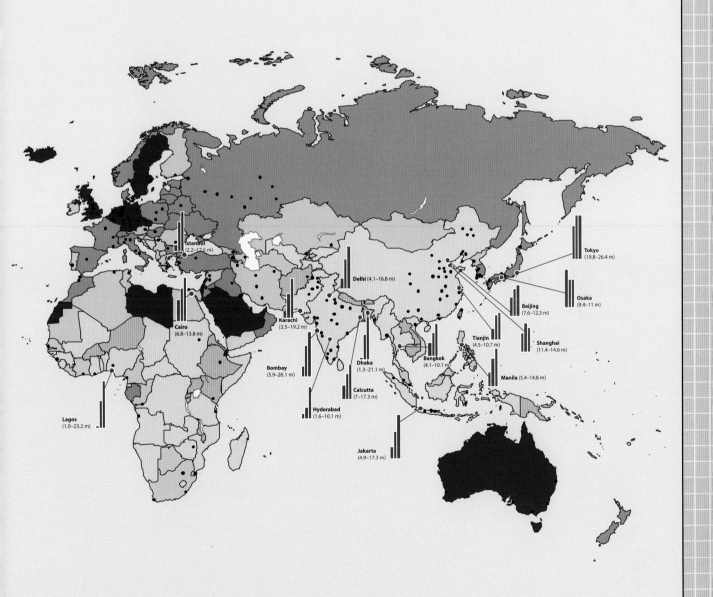

Istanbul
(2.2–12.5 m)

Delhi (4.1–16.8 m)

Cairo
(6.8–13.8 m)

Karachi
(3.5–19.2 m)

Bombay
(5.9–26.1 m)

Hyderabad
(1.6–10.1 m)

Dhaka
(1.3–21.1 m)

Calcutta
(7–17.3 m)

Bangkok
(4.1–10.1 m)

Tianjin
(4.5–10.7 m)

Manila (5.4–14.8 m)

Tokyo
(19.8–26.4 m)

Osaka
(9.4–11 m)

Beijing
(7.6–12.3 m)

Shanghai
(11.4–14.6 m)

Lagos
(1.0–23.2 m)

Jakarta
(4.9–17.3 m)

Charting the World's Cities

Figure 2: Percentage of the World's Population Living in Urban Areas from 1950 to 2030

It is projected that more than 60 percent of the world's population will live in urban areas by 2030. (LA & C = Latin America and the Caribbean; MDR = More Developed Regions)

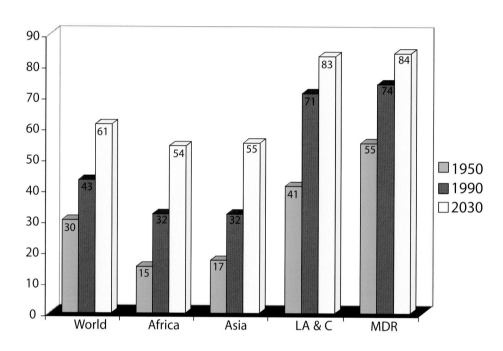

Figure 3: Percentage of the World's Population Not Served by a Supply of Clean Water

Figure 4: Percentage of the World's Population Not Served by Proper Sanitation

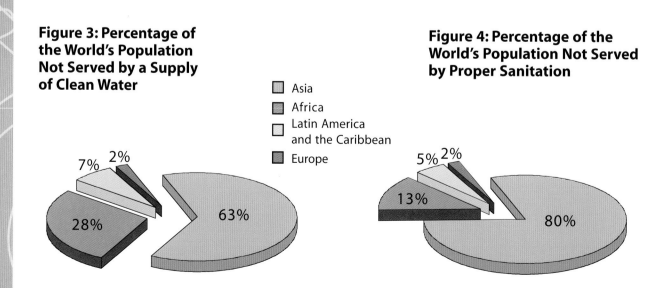

Figure 5: Percentage of Urban and Rural Dwellers with Clean Water in 1990 and 2000

WHO regards clean water as one of the basic elements of good health. It plans to provide clean water to more than 90 percent of the world's population by 2015.

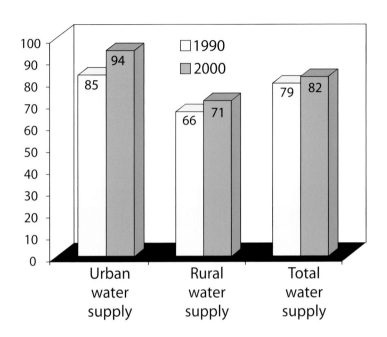

Figure 6: Percentage of Urban and Rural Dwellers with Proper Sanitation in 1990 and 2000

WHO regards proper sanitation as one of the basic elements of good health. It plans to provide proper sanitation to more than 80 percent of the world's population by 2015.

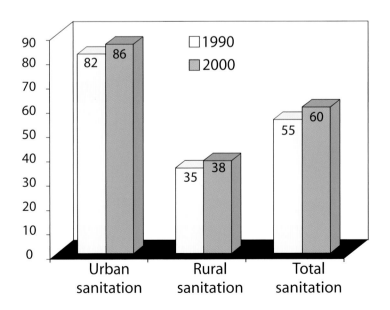

Education for Health

Many of the world's urban poor face extra challenges to stay healthy, and people may not know how to prevent illness. Therefore, health care education is vital. Building hospitals is one way to combat disease, but educating the public, although difficult and time consuming, is ultimately more effective. Urban dwellers must learn the basics of good health practices. These practices may include boiling water, washing food and hands, avoiding drugs, eating healthy food, and practicing safe sex.

Urban populations are threatened by many diseases. Measles, for example, kills one million children a year and

causes complications for millions more. **Tuberculosis** afflicts more than one billion people around the world. Poor water and improper sanitation can cause **schistosomiasis** and diarrhea. Forty million people have HIV/AIDS, a disease of the human immune system. Public health education can help urban dwellers prevent these types of serious diseases.

Public health education also targets injuries. Since injuries at home, on the road, and in the workplace can often be prevented, health education teaches people how to work, drive, and live more safely.

Health education takes resources. It is necessary to train public health educators and develop cheap, effective techniques that people can use to stay healthy. Information must be spread through print, radio, television, and other media, and it must reach adults and children at work, school, and home. Finally, governments have to enforce existing laws concerning public health and make new ones.

Laws can improve public health by preventing injuries. For example, seatbelt laws, speed limits, and bicycle helmet laws protect people involved in traffic accidents. Laws can also reduce injuries caused by violence.

In Cali, Colombia, the leading cause of death among city dwellers in the 1980s was not cancer or heart failure. It was murder. City officials acted to reduce violent crime. They banned weapons such as handguns and knives and restricted the sale of alcohol in public places. In cities around the world, violence is a major health hazard. In the U.S., guns

▰ **Rallies are a safe and visible way to raise awareness of an issue, raise money, voice opposition, and educate the public at the grassroots level.**

kill 40 percent more people than drug use. Guns kill twice as many people as HIV/AIDS. Medical care can treat the results of violence, but it does not prevent it. The health of

---

Medical care can treat the results of violence, but it cannot prevent it.

---

cities may have as much to do with social issues as with medical care.

Problems such as drugs, alcohol, and domestic violence are related to people's values and beliefs. They are part of culture. Unfortunately, changing a culture, whether based in substance abuse or violence, is more difficult than building a hospital.

The victims of domestic violence are usually women and children. Today, public education campaigns are teaching women to help themselves, and more women are getting involved in grassroots organizations. These movements aim to improve women's rights, health, and living conditions.

Children are the long-term answer to cultural change. If they can be taught the importance of community, the environment, and good health habits, there is hope for the future. The Healthy Cities Foundation in Pécs, Hungary, found that children ranked the environment as the country's worst problem.

Two-thirds of them thought that the environment would affect their health in the next 25 years. Environmental awareness is high in Eastern Europe, but there is less environmental awareness in Africa and Latin America. In poorer regions, more immediate concerns, such as getting enough food, are more urgent.

In many cities in the developing world, the poor do not have access to a decent standard of living. They drink polluted water and breathe polluted air. City authorities cannot meet the demand for clean water, proper sanitation, electricity, transportation, jobs, and schools. Children living in these conditions understand the importance of a healthy city environment.

In many cities in the developing world, the poor do not have access to a decent standard of living.

In Tehran, Iran, a Healthy Cities project includes health care training for children. They are encouraged to keep their neighborhoods, homes, and schools clean. A magazine called *Healthy Message* offers ideas for practicing proper hygiene. Iranians have embraced the idea of healthy cities with enthusiasm and skill.

In the quest for healthier cities, city managers, engineers, scientists, and health workers from all over the world are coming together in conferences and meetings. At these meetings, ideas are freely exchanged, and relationships are built. Such meetings are encouraging in a world that often seems divided by conflict.

Volunteers and youth groups who participate in annual cleanups illustrate the importance of individual action in creating healthy environments.

GENDER EMPOWERMENT MEASURE (GEM)

In many ways, urbanization is good for women. Better access to health care makes pregnancy and childbirth safer. There are more education and job opportunities, and women do not need to work as hard to find fuel, food, and water.

Unfortunately, urbanization also creates problems for women. City life carries a higher risk of violence. Basic resources such as food are more expensive, and many women must work in low-paying jobs and in unsafe conditions.

Women must be involved in making cities livable for themselves, and they must be able to influence the policies that affect them. These polices may be political, economic, social, or environmental. In many parts of the world, such participation is impossible for women because some cultures exclude women from public life.

The UN measures women's participation in public life with the Gender Empowerment Measure (GEM). GEM counts how many women hold government seats, which reflects women's involvement in government decisions. It also counts female managers, administrators, professionals, and technical workers, which reveals women's participation in economic decisions. GEM ranks countries based on the influence of women in relation to their proportion of the population. Additional factors determine the ranking system. In 2002, the U.S. was ranked 11th of all countries studied.

GEM Rank	Percentage of Government Seats Held by Women	Percentage of Female Administrators and Managers	Percentage of Female Professional and Technical Workers
1. Norway	36	25	49
2. Iceland	35	27	53
3. Sweden	43	29	49
4. Denmark	38	23	50
5. Finland	37	27	56
6. The Netherlands	33	27	46
7. Canada	24	35	53
8. Germany	31	27	50
9. New Zealand	31	38	54
10. Australia	27	26	48
11. United States	14	45	54
12. Austria	25	28	49
13. Switzerland	22	22	42

Many cities have started campaigns to plant trees. Trees are important to the health of a city. They remove carbon dioxide from the atmosphere and release oxygen. Trees also add to the beauty of a city, which can help reduce the stress caused by living in a large, modern city.

KEY CONCEPTS

Culture Culture refers to beliefs and attitudes. Beliefs and attitudes affect how people act and how they treat others. Often, culture can obstruct good health. In some cases, health educators must try to change people's beliefs and attitudes in order to improve their health. Health educators also teach children the importance of proper health habits, community, and the environment.

Public health Public health deals with the health of the whole community. Public health workers help communities prevent and control disease and injuries. They also teach people how to stay healthy.

Born: May 4, 1916, in Scranton, Pennsylvania
Legacy: Inspires city planners around the world

Navigate to **http://bss.sfsu.edu/ pamuk/urban** to learn more about Jane Jacobs. Also click on **www3.sympatico.ca/ david.macleod/ UTOPS.HTM** to learn more about urban planning.

People in Focus

Jane Jacobs's ideas—and her courage—inspire city planners around the world.

Jacobs was born on May 4, 1916, in Scranton, Pennsylvania. She moved to New York City shortly after graduating from high school and worked as a journalist, writing for the *New York Herald Tribune* and *Vogue* magazine. During World War II, she worked for the Office of War Information. After the war, she continued her career writing for an architecture magazine.

Jacobs is best known for her 1961 book *The Death and Life of Great American Cities*. In it, she argues that U.S. cities are becoming dangerous and depressing places to live. She believes that separating houses from workplaces, schools, and shops isolates people. Jacobs suggests a mixed-use city planning approach. This type of planning locates homes and businesses in the same neighborhood—even in the same building. She feels that cities are more prosperous when people live close together rather than spread out over a large area.

Jacobs is passionate about cities. In 1968, she was arrested in New York City while protesting the building of an expressway. She moved to Toronto, Canada, soon after the protest and her arrest. When the city of Toronto planned an expressway through her new house in 1969, she felt it was necessary to protest once again. Through her writing and public speaking, Jacobs convinced her fellow citizens that neighborhoods should be held together, not divided by expressways. September 7, 1991, was declared Jane Jacobs Day in Toronto. This celebration honored the 30th anniversary of the publication of *The Death and Life of Great American Cities* and recognized Jacobs's role in making Toronto a healthy city.

The Urban Economy

Healthy cities have healthy economies. There must be jobs for all who want to work because unemployment and underemployment cause conflict and illness. Of course, building a strong urban economy is not easy. Each city has its own unique resources and culture, and factors such as these must be considered.

Some businesses are part of the basic infrastructure of a city, and they include the providers of services such as electricity, water, sanitation, waste disposal, road maintenance, and telephone links. Traditionally, such services have been publicly owned, and citizens pay for them through their taxes. But more and more, cities are privatizing some parts or all of these activities. Some city leaders believe that private

Municipalities and private waste collection companies are beginning to require people to separate their recyclables, such as bottles, cans, and newspapers, from the rest of their garbage. Recycling reduces the amount of garbage that goes into landfills.

companies are more efficient than government-run services. Forcing public services to compete with private companies has boosted efficiency in many cases. Also, public-private partnerships have become a popular strategy in urban management. International agencies, such as the UN, are in favor of these partnerships.

Industries bring money to cities, but they also bring pollution. In the past, cities dealt with this problem by locating industries in rural areas. This tactic took jobs away from cities and gave industries no reason to stop polluting. A better strategy is to clean up the industries so they no longer pollute. In this

---

Industries bring money to cities, but they also bring pollution.

---

way, they can operate in cities without causing health problems.

A city's wealth includes human resources as well as money, and urban dwellers can enrich their communities in many ways. Some cities are beginning to use grassroots energy to improve urban life. For example, some people are paid to plant trees in their own neighborhoods. They take better care of the trees than they would if local authorities had planted them. In Minnesota, a program called UNITREE-Tree Keepers gives grants for neighborhood tree planting. Other programs, such as community markets and anti-littering campaigns, allow citizens to take part in improving their communities.

Land ownership is a critical issue in many cities. Often, urban development is informal. This means that people own homes, markets, and businesses built on land they do not legally own. At one time, city authorities would fight these developments. Now, more cities are encouraging them. Cities are giving legal titles to people for the land they use. They are providing services, too. In this way, people without land are able to help themselves and boost the economy.

UN-HABITAT

UN-HABITAT is the UN Human Settlements Program. Its mission is to promote sustainable urbanization. UN-HABITAT works with governments, NGOs, and local authorities. It has three main goals:

1. To improve housing for poor people around the world

2. To help governments work more effectively

3. To encourage countries to work together to solve housing problems

UN-HABITAT uses several strategies to achieve its goals. This program tries to slow the rate of migration from rural to urban areas by taking steps to improve rural life. It also tries to provide the basics for city dwellers. These basics include decent housing, clean water, proper sanitation, disaster prevention, and safe communities.

Some people argue that economic success should come before urban health. According to these people, a city must achieve a certain level of prosperity before it can consider ways to improve its health. For example, Kaohsiung, Taiwan, became wealthy through industrial growth. This growth also damaged the environment, leaving the city unhealthy. Now, Kaohsiung is trying to become a healthy city with its "Kaohsiung 21" project.

Others argue that urban health should come first. When people prosper in a healthy

---

Some people argue that economic success should come before urban health.

---

environment, the city will prosper, too. Cities must balance business, human,

and environmental factors. According to this view, economic growth has consequences for people and the environment, and cities cannot afford to ignore these problems.

Urban health includes many factors. Social well being, health, community pride, and a pleasant environment are just as important to the health of a city as economic wealth.

UNITED STATES AGENCY FOR INTERNATIONAL DEVELOPMENT

United States Agency for International Development (USAID) is a program operated by the United States government. One focus of USAID is to help cities in developing countries become healthier.

Unhealthy cities cause many problems for their citizens. Air pollution causes respiratory illnesses. Poor sanitation and bad water cause disease. People with health problems are less able to earn a living, and sick children neglect their education. The worst areas are crowded inner-city districts and **squatter** communities. New **strains** of diseases develop quickly in such areas. Often, such diseases are difficult or impossible to treat. Visitors, returning tourists, and immigrants can carry these diseases when they enter the United States. These illnesses are becoming more and more prevalent in U.S. communities.

USAID wants to protect U.S. citizens and help people in developing countries. It offers many forms of aid to help cities become healthy. USAID helps city leaders make plans to improve and manage their environments, and it lends its expertise to help create laws and regulations. USAID educates local governments and NGOs through training, exchange visits, and partnerships. It helps communities decide on the best technologies for managing waste, providing water, and other services. USAID also helps cities find ways to pay for the improvements they need.

HEALTHY CITIES PROGRAM

The World Health Organization runs the Healthy Cities and Urban Governance Program. The goal of this program is to support health development in cities and communities. It brings together politicians, experts, and citizens to address urban health issues such as poverty, city planning, access to health care, and the environment.

There are 55 cities in the Healthy Cities Network, and more than 1,300 cities are involved in national healthy cities networks across 30 European countries. WHO works with these cities by providing information, training, and networking. With WHO's help, cities develop Healthy Cities Programs to suit their own needs.

Millions of people live in slums and shantytowns, and they often suffer from serious health problems due to a lack of clean water and proper sanitation.

Men account for the majority of homeless people, but the number of homeless women, children, and youths—estimated to be 40 percent of the total homeless population—has been growing in recent years.

KEY CONCEPTS

Economy Economy refers to the production and distribution of wealth. The formal economy is the official exchange of money for goods and services. In the informal economy, exchanges do not always involve money. Bartering and trading are examples of informal economy.

Industry Industry refers to the production of goods. The manufacture of cars, computers, and clothing are all examples of industry. Industries can be both helpful and harmful to growing cities. On one hand, they provide jobs and attract investors. On the other hand, they can cause pollution and devalue nearby land.

Sustainable development Urbanization affects people and the environment. City planners must consider these factors if a city is to grow sustainably. Sustainable development does not damage the environment. It ensures that people's physical, mental, and social needs are met, and it allows the city's economy to grow and thrive.

Born: December 17, 1937, in Curitiba, Brazil
Legacy: Made Curitiba, Brazil, a model of healthy growth

Navigate to **www.bbc.co.uk/dna/360/A816680** to learn more about Jaime Lerner and Curitiba. Also click on **www.unhabitat.org/programmes/sustainablecities** to learn more about the UN's programs for sustainable cities.

People in Focus

Jaime Lerner made Curitiba, Brazil, a model of healthy growth. Lerner was born in Curitiba on December 17, 1937. In the 1960s, he studied architecture and planning in France. After working in France for a short time, he returned to Curitiba. In 1965, he set up the Research and Urban Planning Institute of Curitiba. Lerner was also part of a team of architects creating a new master plan for Curitiba.

Lerner's political career has been as successful as his planning career. He was mayor of Curitiba three times: from 1971 to 1975, 1979 to 1983, and 1989 to 1992. He was elected governor of Paraná state in 1994 and again in 1998. He also serves as a planning consultant to the UN.

As mayor of Curitiba, Lerner improved the city's infrastructure. He created a bus system that is famous around the world for its efficiency. The bus tickets double as lottery tickets. This transit system has allowed Curitiba to escape the traffic problems common to other growing cities. Lerner also solved the city's flooding problems. He created parks with lakes to hold the extra water. More important, he focused on people and the environment, and he created numerous programs to help the poor. He also found ways to keep the environment clean. As governor of Paraná, Lerner continues to promote social and environmental reforms.

Lerner has been honored around the world for his work. In 1990, he won the United Nations Environmental Award. In 1996, UNICEF presented him with the Child and Peace Award. The University of Virginia awarded him the Thomas Jefferson Medal in 1997.

The Human City

American author Henry David Thoreau once described cities as places where millions of people are lonely together. In a healthy city, this is not the case.

Citizens of healthy cities are able to work and prosper. They do not sit in traffic jams. They know their neighbors, and they feel safe on their streets. Neighborhoods with parks, trees, cafés, shops, and leisure facilities make city life healthy and enjoyable. Healthy cities also have strong economies, good transportation systems, and long-time residents.

Seaside, Florida, is an example of a return to traditional neighborhoods. Seaside has become a model for town and city planners worldwide.

Cities can suffer from various kinds of ill health. Diseases such as cholera, **typhoid**, and **bronchitis** are common in cities in the developing world. In developed countries, cities show signs of social illness. These social ills include crime, homelessness, drug addiction, litter, and vandalism. Social ills are often more difficult to cure than physical ills.

Today, much is known about how physical and social factors are linked and how they affect health. For example, the stress caused by living and working in a large, crowded city can affect a person's health. Fortunately, there are several ways to reduce stress and make city life healthier. Building houses, schools, and workplaces close together makes long car trips unnecessary. Houses with front porches invite more friendly exchanges between people than houses with front driveways. Clean, well-lit streets with plenty of trees make walking safe and pleasant.

In Malaysia, the prime minister's office runs a Healthy Cities Program. The city of Kuching shows how the program can work for a small city. Kuching officials asked citizens to share ideas for improving the city. They used this feedback to improve local transportation, housing, and schools. Kuching's Healthy Cities activities focus on keeping the nearby Sarawak River clean, keeping the city beautiful, and preventing crime. The city sponsors a "Beautification and Cleanliness" competition. There are also

---

Healthy cities have strong economies, good transportation systems, and long-time residents.

---

road safety and crime prevention programs. Thousands of cities around the world could learn from the example of Kuching.

In Chittagong, Bangladesh, the Healthy Cities Program asks the city's poor to participate. In the past, city officials had never thought to ask the people what they wanted. Everyone thought the authorities knew what was best for them. Now, there is a Slum Dwellers **Forum**. The forum represents more than one million people living in the city's slum areas.

For many cities, such multi-level participation is a novelty. There may be great resistance to involving certain groups in decision making or planning. The experiences of Kuching and Chittagong show that a healthy city is one where all citizens feel the city belongs to them. Failure to meet the needs of all interest groups puts a city's health at risk.

For the world's mega-cities, it may be too late for such grand visions. In cities of 10 to 20 million people, it is hard for governments to make sweeping changes. However, if urban planning is open and fair and local people are encouraged to pursue their own improvement projects, even mega-cities can become healthy places for people to live and work.

SEASIDE, FLORIDA

Seaside is an example of how new settlements can avoid the pitfalls of big cities. Seaside was designed in 1981, and its developers have tried to recapture the feel of traditional U.S. towns.

The town encourages neighbors to get to know each other. Each house has a front porch, and downtown was created as a marketplace where people buy and sell food and crafts.

Seaside favors walking rather than traffic jams. Workplaces, schools, shops, and entertainment are within walking distance of homes. The streets are designed to make walking more convenient than driving.

Seaside's planners and residents hope to recapture an era when neighbors chatted over the fence and children played in the streets. The town illustrates how planning can enhance the social health of a community.

CHATTANOOGA, TENNESSEE

In 1969, Chattanooga, Tennessee, had the worst air pollution in the United States, so Chattanoogans decided to do something about it. Government, industry, health professionals, and citizens cooperated to solve the problem. The city adopted higher air quality standards, and industries reduced their pollution. As a result of these efforts, Chattanooga's air quality improved.

But the changes did not stop there. Throughout the 1980s, the city continued its makeover. Chattanooga's leaders asked the citizens what changes should be made. People suggested improvements to the city's public spaces. These projects include a big-screen theater, an aquarium, and the Riverwalk, a pedestrian path along the river.

The Riverwalk is a good example of urban health. It preserves the area's natural environment, and it is a meeting place for walkers, joggers, cyclists, and fishers. The Riverwalk enhances the physical and social well being of Chattanooga's citizens.

Urban sprawl destroys farmlands, open spaces, and wetlands. It also contributes to social problems such as crime.

WHAT MAKES A HEALTHY CITY?

According to the World Health Organization (WHO), a healthy city:

- is clean and safe;

- provides safe food, clean water, energy, and proper sanitation;

- has a strong economy that provides adequate jobs, goods, and services;

- works with organizations to improve health;

- involves citizens in the decision-making process;

- provides entertainment and leisure activities where citizens can meet;

- values its history and cultural diversity;

- provides accessible and good-quality health services; and

- is located in a sustainable ecosystem.

Based on these points, how many of the world's cities do you think are healthy?

KEY CONCEPTS

City planning City or urban planning is the design of cities and services. City planning involves deciding where various sectors of a city should go and how to provide services for them. Good planning considers the needs of a city's residents, businesses, visitors, and service providers. It should also take into account how a city will grow and change in the future.

Public, semi-private, and private spaces Spaces in a city can be public, semi-private, or private. Public spaces are places where everyone has a right to go. These spaces are usually owned by the citizens themselves. Streets, parks, town squares, and city halls are examples of public spaces. Semi-private spaces are public spaces with private owners.

Shopping malls and office buildings are semi-private spaces. People can usually enter semi-private spaces, but the owners or occupants have the right to ask anyone to leave. Private spaces are people's homes and yards. People need an invitation or permission from the owner to enter private spaces.

Time Line of Events

1900
Only 14 percent of the world's people live in cities.

1909
The First National Conference on City Planning is held in Washington, D.C.

1916
Jane Jacobs, known for her book *The Death and Life of Great American Cities*, is born in Scranton, Pennsylvania.

1937
Jaime Lerner, known for his innovative city planning, is born in Curitiba, Brazil.

1940
Only New York and London have populations of more than five million people.

1945
The United Nations (UN) is founded.

1948
The World Health Organization (WHO) is founded.

1950
One-third of the world's people live in cities.

1961
The Death and Life of Great American Cities, by Jane Jacobs, is published.

1971
Jaime Lerner is elected mayor of Curitiba for the first of three terms.

1975
In the developing world, 110 cities have more than one million people. In developed countries, 85 cities have more than one million people.

1976
Habitat I, the first United Nations Conference on Human Settlements, takes place in Vancouver, Canada.

1984
Construction begins on Seaside, Florida.

1986
WHO launches the Healthy Cities Program in Europe.

1987
The Mega-Cities Project is launched.

1990
Thirty cities have populations of more than five million.

1993–1999
President's Council on Sustainable Development advises President Clinton on development issues.

1995
In the developing world, 250 cities have more than one million people. In developed countries, 114 cities have more than one million people.

1996
Habitat II, the second UN Conference on Human Settlements, takes place in Istanbul, Turkey.

■■■■■ **Habitat for Humanity International, which was founded in 1976, has built or renovated more than 125,000 homes for families in need.**

1998

In the United States, there are 27 million poor urban dwellers and 7.5 million poor rural residents.

2000

There are 17 mega-cities in the world.

2000

Tokyo is the world's largest city, with more than 24 million people living in it.

2001

The United States ranks 6th on the UN's Human Development Index. It ranks 17th on the Human Poverty Index.

2002

More than one billion people do not have access to clean water.

2005 (projected)

Half of the world's people will live in cities.

2015 (projected)

There may be as many as 10 new mega-cities. New York and Los Angeles will become mega-cities.

2030 (projected)

Sixty percent of the world's people will live in cities.

Concept Web

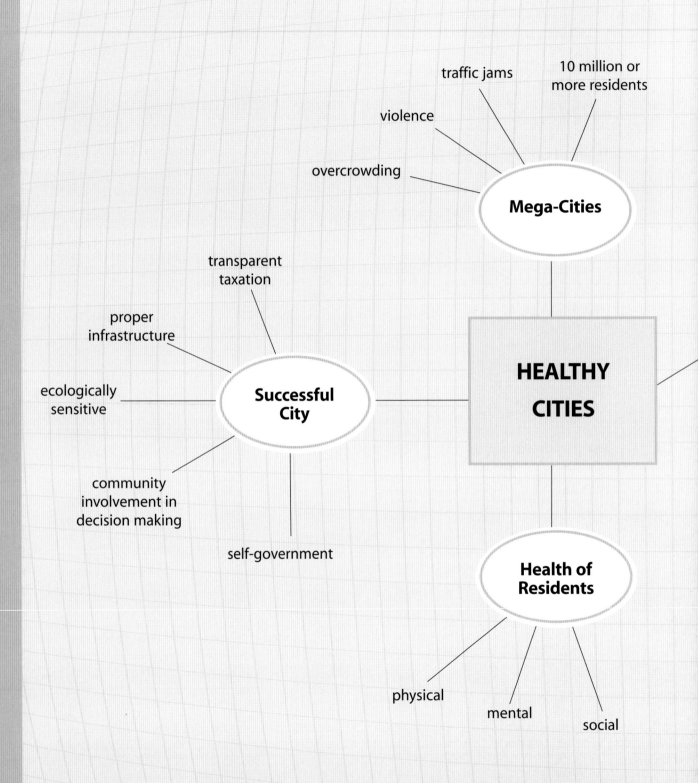

traffic jams

10 million or more residents

violence

overcrowding

Mega-Cities

transparent taxation

proper infrastructure

ecologically sensitive

Successful City

community involvement in decision making

self-government

HEALTHY CITIES

Health of Residents

physical

mental

social

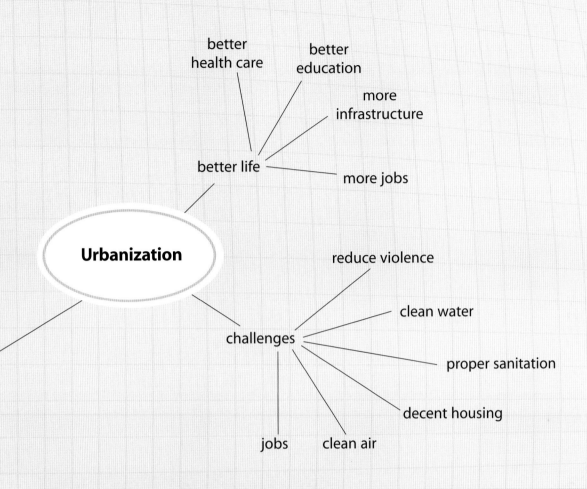

better health care

better education

more infrastructure

better life

more jobs

Urbanization

reduce violence

clean water

challenges

proper sanitation

decent housing

jobs

clean air

MAKE YOUR OWN CONCEPT WEB

A concept web is a useful summary tool. It can also be used to plan your research or help you write an essay or report. To make your own concept web, follow the steps below.

- You will need a large piece of unlined paper and a pencil.
- First, read through your source material, such as *Healthy Cities: Improving Urban Life* in the Understanding Global Issues series.
- Write the main idea, or concept, in large letters in the center of the page.
- On a sheet of lined paper, jot down all words, phrases, or lists that you know are connected with the concept. Try to do this from memory.
- Look at your list. Can you group your words and phrases in certain topics or themes? Connect the different topics with lines to the center or to other "branches."
- Critique your concept web. Ask questions about the material on your concept web: Does it all make sense? Are all the links shown? Could there be other ways of looking at it? Is anything missing?
- What more do you need to find out? Develop questions for those areas you are still unsure about or where information is missing. Use these questions as a basis for further research.

Quiz

Multiple Choice

1. Curitiba's mayor, Jaime Lerner, paid attention to what urban issue?
   a) transportation
   b) social issues
   c) the environment
   d) all of the above

2. The houses of Seaside, Florida:
   a) are surrounded by high fences
   b) have large concrete driveways
   c) have front porches
   d) are protected by armed guards

3. WHO stands for:
   a) World Health Organization
   b) White-Haired Orangutans
   c) World Humanity Order
   d) Worldwide Hunger Opposition

4. In healthy cities, decisions are made by:
   a) government only
   b) government and business
   c) citizens only
   d) government, business, and citizens

5. Urbanization is:
   a) the movement of people from cities to rural areas
   b) cities with more than one million residents
   c) the movement of people from rural areas to cities
   d) a sustainable city

Where Did It Happen?

1. It is a model for cities trying to cope with the pressures of urbanization.
2. The Industrial Revolution began here in the 1700s.
3. This part of the world spends $11 billion a year on ice cream.
4. The Communal Whole Foods Program is operated in this city.
5. This state has passed laws to increase the number of zero-emission vehicles on its roads.

True or False

1. A mega-city has fewer than 10 million residents.
2. Jane Jacobs was arrested in New York.
3. "Healthy cities" refers only to disease control.
4. The United States ranks first overall on the UN's Human Development Index (HDI).
5. A city planner deals with rodent control, food safety, and hazardous materials.

Answers on page 53

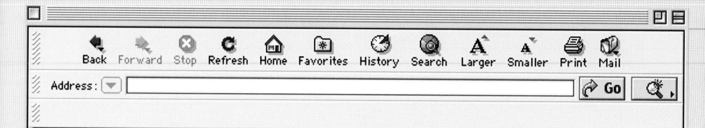

Internet Resources

The following organizations are devoted to issues and education about urbanization and development:

The Mega-cities Project
http://www.megacitiesproject.org
The Mega-cities Project helps the world's largest cities stay healthy and livable. This Web site features a video, a newsletter, and profiles of the world's largest cities.

UN-HABITAT
http://www.unhabitat.org
UN-HABITAT is the United Nations Human Settlements Program. This branch of the UN helps governments deal with the pressures of urbanization. This Web site features news and highlights of urban development. Users can register on the site to receive newsletters.

United States Agency for International Development (USAID)
http://www.usaid.gov
USAID offers assistance to governments and NGOs in the developing world. This Web site has information about USAID projects around the world. Visitors can search by topic or by region.

Some Web sites stay current longer than others. To find other Web sites, enter terms such as "cities," "mega-cities," or "population" into a search engine.

Further Reading

Evans, Peter. *Livable Cities? Urban Struggles for Livelihood and Sustainability.* Berkeley, CA: University of California Press, 2002.

Foo, A. F., and Belinda Yuen. *Sustainable Cities in the 21st Century.* Singapore: National University of Singapore, 1999.

Hall, Peter, and Ulrich Pfeiffer. *Urban Future 21: A Global Agenda for 21st Century Cities.* New York: E & FN Spon, 2000.

Jacobs, Jane. *The Death and Life of Great American Cities.* New York: Random House, 1961.

McGranahan, Gordon. *The Citizens at Risk: From Urban Sanitation to Sustainable Cities.* London: Earthscan Publications, 2001.

Portney, Kent E. *Taking Sustainable Cities Seriously: Economic Development, the Environment, and Quality of Life in American Cities.* Cambridge, MA: MIT Press, 2003.

United Nations Center for Human Settlements. *Cities in a Globalizing World: Global Report on Human Settlements 2001.* Sterling, VA: Earthscan Publications, 2001.

Answers

Multiple Choice
  1. d) 2. c) 3. a) 4. d) 5. c)

Where Did It Happen?
  1. Curitiba, Brazil 2. England 3. Europe 4. Buenos Aires 5. California

True or False
  1. F 2. T 3. F 4. F 5. F

Glossary

bronchitis: a disease of the lungs, often made worse by air pollution

cholera: a disease, sometimes fatal, caused by contaminated food or water

communism: a system within which all possessions are owned equally by all citizens

contaminated: polluted with harmful substances

decentralization: the delegation of power from a central authority to regional and local authorities

developed countries: countries with strong social and economic conditions

developing countries: poorer countries in the process of improving social and economic conditions

emissions: fumes from the burning of fuel or other substances

forum: a meeting where a public discussion is held

hepatitis: a disease of the liver, often caused by contaminated food or water

holistic: a way of problem solving that considers the whole problem rather than breaking it into parts

infrastructure: the systems that operate in a city, such as transportation, power, water, and sanitation systems

metropolitan: having to do with large cities and the areas around them

municipal: concerning the government of a city or town

per capita: per person

practitioners: people who work in a profession

prosperity: wealth; economic success

rickshaw: a small passenger vehicle with two wheels that is usually pulled by one person

sanitation: the protection of public health by the proper disposal of sewage

schistosomiasis: a disease caused by a parasite that lives in untreated water

solar panels: a group of connected solar cells that convert sunlight into electricity

solar power: energy from the sun

squatter: a person who lives on property without owning or paying for it

strains: types or variations of a disease

tuberculosis: a disease of the lungs, often spread by poor living conditions

typhoid: an infectious disease spread through contaminated food or water

underemployed: working at a job that is below the subsistence level

zero-emission: industrial processes that do not produce harmful emissions

Index

Photo Credits

Cover: Lavender Bay, Sydney, Australia (**MaXx Images**); **Corel Corporation**: pages 1, 9; **Digital Vision, Ltd.**: pages 4, 10/11, 20, 24, 45TL, 45TR, 45M; **Government of the State of Paraná**: page 41; **Habitat for Humanity**: page 47; **John J. Burns Library, Boston College**: page 35; **Lampo Communication Inc.**: pages 2/3; **Bruce Leighty**: pages 23, 44; **MaXx Images**: pages 15, 36/37; **Panos Pictures**: pages 38/39 (**Jeremy Horner**); **PhotoDisc, Inc.**: page 21; **Seaside, Florida**: page 42; **George Sidney Shepherd/Getty Images**: page 6; **Tom Stack & Associates**: pages 16 (**Thomas Kitchin**), 34 (**Chip and Jill Isenhart**); **Visuals Unlimited**: pages 13, 18, 30, 40 (**Jeff Greenberg**), 32 (**Ted Whittenkraus**); **World Health Organization**: page 14 (**Pierre Virot**).